Potty Training il.

DATE DUE

A Guide For Today's Parents

A Mom Innovations Book

www.Potty-Training-in-One-Day.com

Narmin Parpia

Potty Training in One Day
A Guide for Today's Parents
Featuring Potty Scotty™ and Potty Patty®

Potty Training is one of the most challenging processes a parent faces. For some parents, this is a rewarding and memorable experience, while for others it can be a frustrating time. This book walks parents through the entire potty process — from determining if their child is ready, to how to handle bowel movement training and bedwetting. It answers common questions such as:

At what age should I start potty training?
How do I know if my child is ready to be potty trained?
What should I do? How should I potty train?
What does potty training in one day mean?
What about Bowel Movement Training?
What should I do if my child resists training?
How do I handle night time potty training and bed wetting?

… and much more. My goal is to help parents prepare for this important developmental milestone and make it a positive and memorable experience for both parent and child.

Narmin Parpia
Potty Training in One Day™
6905 Broadway, Suite 203
Pearland, TX 77581
www.Potty-Training-in-One-Day.com
narmin@Potty-Training-in-One-Day.com

Requests for Information should be addressed to:
Mom Innovations
6905 Broadway, Suite 203
Pearland, TX 77581

Potty Training In One Day: A Guide For Today's Parents
ISBN 0-9779054-0-3

Printed in the United States of America

Table Of Contents

DEDICATION ix

ACKNOWLEDGMENTS xi

PLEASE NOTE xii

INTRODUCTION xv

SECTION I: POTTY TRAINING TODAY 1

POTTY TRAINING METHODS 3

    I.   THE INFANT POTTY TRAINING OR 3
           ELIMINATION COMMUNICATION METHOD

    II.   CHILD ORIENTED PRESSURE-FREE APPROACH 4

    III. PRACTICE MAKES PERFECT 5

    IV. THE NAKED & $75 METHOD 7

    V.   THE POTTY TRAINING IN ONE DAY METHOD 8

SECTION II: PREPARATION AND PLANNING 13

IS YOUR CHILD READY TO POTTY TRAIN? 14

    1. PHYSIOLOGICAL DEVELOPMENT READINESS 15

    2. MOTOR SKILLS DEVELOPMENT READINESS 16

    3. COGNITIVE AND VERBAL SKILLS READINESS 17

    4. EMOTIONAL GROWTH AND SOCIAL 18
       AWARENESS READINESS

READINESS SIGNALS SUMMARIZED 19

ARE YOU READY? 21

SOME DO'S AND DON'TS OF 23
POTTY TRAINING

REQUIRED POTTY TRAINING 26
EQUIPMENT
SELECTING THE BIG DAY 33

SECTION III: THE BIG DAY 35
THE GROWING UP CEREMONY 37
LEARNING DESIRED BEHAVIORS AND 38
CONSEQUENCES
LEARNING UNDESIRED BEHAVIORS 45
AND CONSEQUENCES
AFTER GOAL ACHIEVEMENT 49

SECTION IV: FOLLOW UP & MAINTENANCE 51
SHOULD YOU EVER USE PULL-ONS 54
DURING THE DAY?
WHAT ABOUT NAPTIME? 54
NIGHT TIME POTTY TRAINING.............................55
LEAVING THE HOUSE – BACK TO...............59
NORMAL LIFE
FEAR OF PUBLIC RESTROOMS 61
POTTY TRAINING RESISTANCE.............................61

SECTION V: KEY ISSUES FOR POTTY 65
                TRAINING IN ONE DAY
CHILD HAS NOT INITIATED.........................65
POTTY TRAINING
WHY DO PRACTICE RUNS?.........................68

WHAT IF YOUR CHILD URINATES 69
IN THE POTTY WHILE DOING PRACTICE RUNS?
WHAT IF PRACTICE RUNS ARE NOT............................69
A DETERRENT?
WHAT IF YOUR CHILD GETS 70
JEALOUS OF THE DOLL?

SECTION VI: BOWEL MOVEMENT 73
TRAINING
YOUR CHILD'S BM SCHEDULE...............................74
CHANGE IN BM SCHEDULE 76
CONSTIPATION 77
HOW DO YOU KNOW IF YOUR CHILD 77
IS CONSTIPATED?
HOW DOES CONSTIPATION GET STARTED?...........78
SOILING OR ENCOPRESIS 79
DEALING WITH BM RESISTANCE 83

SECTION VII: BED WETTING 87
TREATING SECONDARY NOCTURNAL 88
ENURESIS
TREATMENT OPTIONS FOR BED WETTING 90
BEHAVIORAL THERAPIES 90
    MOTIVATION PROGRAMS 91
    GUIDED IMAGERY 91
    HYPNOTHERAPY 92
CONDITIONAL THERAPIES 92
    RETENTION CONTROL TRAINING 93

Night-lifting 93
BED WETTING MEDICATION 94
Imipramine (Janimine, Tofranil) 95
Desmopressin (DDAVP, Stimate) 95
Oxybutynin (Ditropan) 96

SECTION VIII - POTTY TRAINING SUMMARY........99

Dedicated To:

My sons
Ryan & Kevin
My two very special gifts from God, who as toddlers proved that you can indeed potty train in one day!

Acknowledgments

I thank God for always being in my life, for guiding me and for showing me the way. My parents – who molded me into the person I am and Mom, thanks for passing down your personality traits.

Dr. Phil McGraw for not only giving me the idea, but for inspiring me to follow my dreams, conquer my fears and be my authentic self.

All the customers who have praised the first three versions of this book and who provided me with the courage and encouragement to publish it. Raj Ramlal, my husband and best friend – for always supporting me and helping me pursue my dreams (even when you did not share my vision). Shairoz Rajwani – my dearest sister - for always being there for me – to listen, care, help and provide encouragement when I need it the most. Michaelyn Dunaway – for telling me things that I do not want to hear, but need to and for all your wisdom and advice. Dr. Samir P. Desai - for sharing your writing and publishing experiences with me. Jennifer Fails – my dear friend – for being there for me, Carol Thelen for reading and providing me with feedback on the initial versions of this book. Kenya Dixon for helping me get started and for your continued support. Gabe – for your photographs. Ava Graves for helping me move closer to my goal, Anita Bunkley for your incredible editing and Marvin D. Cloud for putting the final finishing touches.

Catherine Bryan, Anne Marie Kemp, Liz Siarkowski, Clare Lowther - the girlfriends in my life - who are there for me, who listen to me even when I am boring them to tears, and who provide me with the support and encouragement I need.

Please Note:

This potty training guide and information is written <u>without</u> consideration for any mental, physical or medical conditions. If you suspect your child of having any of these conditions, please consult your physician.

This book and the information in it is intended to compliment, NOT substitute for, the advice of your child's pediatrician. It should not be used as an alternative to appropriate medical care. The author has made every effort to ensure that the information in this book is accurate up to the time of publication. However, in light of ongoing research and the constant flow of information, it is possible that new findings may invalidate some of the data presented here.

Before starting any medical treatment or a new program, you should consult with your own pediatrician, who can discuss your individual needs and counsel you about symptoms and treatment. If you have any questions regarding how the information in this book applies to your child, speak with your child's pediatrician.

The information and advice in this book apply equally to children of both sexes (except where noted). To indicate this, we have chosen to alternate between masculine and feminine pronouns throughout the book.

Introduction

While watching the Dr. Phil show on "How to Potty Train Your Child in One Day" I was reminded of the time I potty trained my boys. They are now 14 and 11 years-old, and I had successfully potty trained both of my children using the book *Toilet Training in Less Than a Day* by two psychologists, Nathan H. Azrin, Ph.D. and Richard M. Foxx, Ph.D.

I trained my oldest son in one day, with only four accidents over a three day period. My second child had zero accidents, and went from diapers to "big kid" underwear without any problems.

The concept behind the "One Day" method is to use a doll that drinks and wets in order to demonstrate "going potty" behavior for your child, and to allow your child to learn to go potty by teaching the doll to do the same. As I recalled the hurdles I had gone through in order to achieve success with my sons, I remembered that my biggest challenge had been locating the necessary supplies — especially a boy doll that would drink and wet.

I eventually found a drink and wet girl doll, (never did find a boy doll) but it had a straight tube from the mouth to the bottom, allowing all of the liquid to immediately drain out. Also, the female doll I had purchased did not have any underwear, so I had to sew some panties for her.

My experience led me to inventing anatomically correct dolls that drink and wet-on-demand™. Along with the dolls, we created a full line of specially designed potty training products - *Potty Scotty*™ products for boys and *Potty Patty*® products for girls.

Our feature products are called *"The Potty Scotty*™ *Kit," "The Potty Patty*® *Kit"* and *"Potty Training in One Day – The Complete System for Boys*™ *or for Girls*®*."* The complete system includes everything a parent would need to potty train in one day.

The *Potty Scotty*™ or *Potty Patty*® Kits include the potty training dolls, bottles for the dolls, "big kid" underwear for the doll and this potty training book. *Potty Training in One Day - The Complete System for Boys*™ *or for Girls*® also includes a potty chair, a toilet/potty seat and 6 pairs of "big kid" potty training underwear for your child.

Other *Potty Scotty*™ and *Potty Patty*® products include waterproof potty training underwear for nap time and night-time, mattress pad, musical potty chair, travel potty chair, potty seats, a urinal for boys and many other potty training aids.

Visit www.PottyScotty.com or www.PottyPatty.com to get

more information and to see the full list of products available.

The information in this book is based on my research, my knowledge and experience, and that of many friends, experts and parents. I truly hope you find this book to be an easy, informational read. I would love to hear from you. Send your comments and feedback to me at www.Potty-Training-in-One-Day.com.

Good Luck!
Narmin Parpia

Potty Training Today

Note: *This potty training guide and information is written <u>without</u> consideration for any mental, physical or medical conditions. If you suspect your child of having any of these conditions, please consult your physician.*

So, is it potty training or potty learning? Some experts prefer to use the words potty learning because it supports the notion that this is a developmental skill that is learned by the child at his own pace and in his own way. I think that it is a little of both. Your child has to learn this developmental skill and your job as the parent is to teach your toddler what to do and what not to do. I choose to use the words potty training because I think that this term is most familiar to parents.

What does potty training mean to you? Most parents will agree that a child who is "potty trained" is using a potty or the toilet and is wearing underwear. My definition of a "potty trained" child is one who is wearing cloth underwear (washable

1

– not disposable) and will initiate using the potty or the toilet when the child has the need to eliminate. However, it is very difficult to get parents to agree on the best way to move from diapers to underwear. There are many ways and approaches to potty training. My favorite technique - Potty Training in One Day — is one potential way of getting there.

Potty training is a developmental skill similar to crawling, walking and talking. Your toddler will learn this skill when he is ready. Just as you encouraged and supported your child in his efforts to walk, you will help your child learn how to potty independently. In North America, the average age for toilet training is 29 months (for bowel training) and 32 months (for bladder), but the range in normal children varies from about 18 to 60 months.

What matters most is not *when* the child meets the challenge, but *how* he and you resolve it. It's his job to do it and it's yours to teach and encourage him. Try not to let it become a power struggle.

Potty training or potty learning is a complicated process. Your child has to make a mental connection with his internal body signals, control his muscles to hold back urination until he gets to the potty, then get his clothes off, sit on the potty chair and then relax the muscles to actually go potty. Looking at the potty training process from a child's perspective, you are asking your child to learn a number of steps, connect them all together and execute them in perfect synchronicity.

Children are very capable of learning all of these steps and pulling them together, however, like all other skills, some children learn these steps easily and effortlessly, while others need more time and effort.

Potty Training Methods

As mentioned earlier, there are many different methods for potty training. Based on my research, there are five different methods or techniques for potty training. I will briefly discuss the other four methods, including the benefits and drawbacks and then I will get into how to potty train in one day in detail.

I. The Infant Potty Training or Elimination Communication Method

This method is most used in underdeveloped nations and probably the least used potty training method in North America. This age-old method operates under the premise that early exposure and consistent practice help children master new skills.

Parents begin when the baby is a few week old by holding the infant over a potty to catch the eliminations. Parents learn the infant's rhythms and the infant learns to recognize physical sensations that precede elimination. This is very effective when disposable diaper use is minimal or nonexistent.

Benefits	Drawbacks
Parent-child bonding.	Time consuming; nearly impossible for working mothers.
Start early, finish early.	
Wetting and soiling are not likely to become entrenched habits.	Have to stay on top of it and stick with it until child can potty independently.
Limited use of diapers results in:	
• Cost effectiveness	Increased accidents and accident clean up.
• Prevention of diaper rash	
• No harm to the environment	
• More hygienic	

II. Child Oriented Pressure-Free Approach

This method is recommended by Dr. Terry Brazelton, who states that "we need to initiate the process with utmost respect for the child – and for his ultimate decision to comply. Training a small child to use the toilet must be taken in steps that respect his willingness to cooperate."

According to Dr. Brazelton, if your child uses the potty, "don't go overboard. Let her know in a calm voice that that was what you had in mind … be calm, no matter how thrilled you are. If you get too excited you'll overwhelm her."

The steps in this method are:

1. Take your child to the store and let him pick out the potty chair.

4

2. Let your child get used to sitting on the potty fully clothed.

3. Empty child's diaper in the potty.

4. The big step – let the child run around bare bottomed.

5. Let your child be involved in his own success, offer potty training panties that he can pull up and down.

Benefits	Drawbacks
Very easy to fit into a busy lifestyle.	Could take from 1 6 months or longer in many cases.
Very little preparation required on the part of the parent.	Child may be quite old before he is ready.
Does not require a large time commitment or consistency from parent; therefore ideal for working parents.	The average age for potty training is going up every year. Dr. Brazelton does not consider age four to be late for training; his input was part of the reason for developing Size 6 (over 35 lbs) in diaper size.
	Wetting and soiling can become entrenched habits for children.

III. Practice Makes Perfect

Most of the books available for parents today suggest some form of this method, and it is probably the hardest method to summarize because it is a combination of concepts and tools that are used for potty training. The common theme among all the books on the subject is that the practice makes perfect.

The concepts and tools suggested are:

1. Introduce the potty to your child and have the potty accessible.

2. Demonstrate "going potty" behavior by having the toddler observe parents, siblings or a potty doll.

3. Parents record the child's going potty schedule and then place the child on the potty based on his potty schedule.

4. Gradually teach him to use the potty chair by holding regular practice sessions. Some books recommend practice sessions can be held once a day, some twice a day. Other books recommend a much more intense schedule; a range of every 15 to 30 minutes depending on the expert.

5. The best way for a child to learn is for him to go in the potty successfully and see the parent's positive reaction.

6. Reward the child. Use stickers and a chart, or give stickers for sitting on the potty and candy for using the potty. This creates a positive support system that encourages the child to sit and use the potty.

7. Track the accidents on a separate private chart, so that the parents can monitor the child's progress.

8. Gradually transition from diapers, to potty, to underwear or ditch the diapers and move directly to potty training pants.

Benefits	Drawbacks
This method can easily fit into a family's busy schedule. With some planning, some structure can be created around the practice sessions - i.e. in the morning and in the evening. Is done gradually over time. Very limited accidents, if any.	Sticking to the structure and schedule until the toddler is potty trained could take anywhere from a weekend to a few months, depending on the child's maturity level, temperament and readiness. May not learn to initiate by himself, because parent always initiates. Difficult to keep the curious toddler interested long enough to sit on the potty and relax until he is able to eliminate.

IV. The Naked & $75 Method

John Rosemond, a family psychologist, columnist and author is the person behind this method. He believes that potty training should be as simple and straight forward as housebreaking a puppy.

The method is very simple:

1. Parents spend three to five consecutive days on the train-

ing method.

2. The child should be between the ages of 24 to 30 months.

3. The child is allowed to be naked all day, with a potty available at all times and correct mistakes matter-of-factly.

Benefits	Drawbacks
Simple, easy and inexpensive.	Not supported by experts.
Quick - 3-5 days.	Messy.

It is important to note that many experts disagree with Rosemond's approach. By the way, the $75 is for the inevitable carpet cleaning.

Go to www.Potty-Training-in-One-Day.com for more information, resources and links on these and other training methods.

V. The Potty Training in One Day Method

Potty Training in One Day — Sounds great, doesn't it? Or does it sound too good to be true? It all comes down to perspective and expectations. Potty Training in One Day is a proven method for potty training children and has successfully potty trained thousands of children over the last 30 years — including my two children.

This method is based on two simple concepts:

1. The best way to learn something is to teach it and/or teaching is the highest form of understanding. A potty training doll will model the appropriate potty training behavior for your child.

2. Behavior is shaped by consequence. Every action has consequences; some consequences are natural, while others are logical.

Let's look at these two concepts more closely:

The first concept is based on the fact that the best way to learn something is to teach it. We know that children learn from seeing, listening and hearing. They learn action and attitudes and will copy things that they have seen. As the parent, you will show your child how to teach a potty training doll the appropriate behaviors for using the potty. With your guidance, your child will take a potty doll through all the steps required to urinate in a potty chair or the toilet.

Not only will you teach your child the behaviors that are desirable, you will also be able to teach him what behaviors are not desirable. Your child will use the potty training doll to model the appropriate going potty behaviors and show you that he truly understands what you expect him to do.

The second concept is based on the fact that behavior is shaped by consequence. As a parent, you already know that children learn from the consequences of their actions and you probably have already used this as an effective parenting tool.

There are two types of consequences for actions – logical and natural. Natural consequence results from the child's own actions. Logical consequence is also a result of behavior, but is imposed by the parent. As you teach your child desired and un-desired behaviors, you will also teach him that all behaviors have consequences. Some behaviors have natural consequences – like drinking a lot of fluids leads to the need to use the potty; while other behaviors have natural, as well as logical consequences — i.e. not urinating in the potty leads to wet underwear, which leads to having to do some practice runs.

As you go through this method, your child will have a clear understanding of the expected behaviors and the consequences of these behaviors.

Benefits	Drawbacks
Quick - can be done in less than one day to a maximum of two weeks	Takes planning and preparation.
Is a structured method. A proven method - developed by Azrin & Foxx over 30 years ago and made popular by Dr. Phil.	Is a structured method.
	Requires follow-through by parents.
Potty Scotty™ and Potty Patty® products provide the tools to support the method.	Made to look easier than it is.

The Potty Training in One Day Process has **Three Distinct Steps** that you will follow. See figure 1 below:

1. Preparation and Planning

2. The Big Day

3. Follow-up

Step 3
Follow Up &
Maintenance

Step 2
The "Big Day"

Step 1
The Planning &
Preparation

Takes 0 – 2 wks, depending on the child and the parents.

Takes 1 day or less.

Takes 1 hr to 2 wks or more, depending on readiness.

Figure 1.

In order for you to have a pleasant and successful "Big Day" you will have to spend some time preparing and planning for this day. The planning and preparation could take anywhere from one hour to a few weeks, depending on how ready you and your child are. The "Big Day" is the "One Day" in Potty Training in One Day and is the day when you will potty train your child. The time required for the follow-up after the "Big Day" really depends on your child. Some children do not require any follow-up, but others may require more.

SECTION II

Preparation And Planning

Know and understand that, on the whole, potty training in one day is a fairly simple and straightforward method; however, it all depends on you and your child. Some children are very easy to train and others are a little more challenging. Some parents love this method and others may not. So be prepared and have a realistic understanding of the process. You have to be willing to follow it as it is outlined. Making modifications that better suit you may work for you, but they also may not. The process as outlined will work if you follow all the steps.

Most importantly, position yourself for success by making sure that both you and your child are ready to do this and that you have everything you will need. My recommendation is that you read this entire book before you start to potty train your child.

Is Your Child Ready To Potty Train?

So you have decided to potty train your child, but is your child ready to be trained? Most children begin to show readiness signs between 20 and 30 months, however, there are others that are not ready until well into their 4th year.

Each child is an individual and has her own rate of physical and mental development, and like all other developmental skills (crawling, walking and talking), toilet training is a skill that your toddler will learn when she is ready. Starting too early may lead to frustration for both the parent and the child: It is like asking a child to crawl, talk or walk before she is ready. Ensuring that your child is ready will not only pave the path for success, but it will also make for a pleasant experience for both parent and child. It will also boost the child's ego and make her proud of her achievement.

There is no set age at which potty training or toilet training should begin. The right time depends on your child's development in the following four areas:

1. Physiological development (bladder and bowel control).

2. Motor skills.

3. Cognitive and verbal development.

4. Emotional and social awareness.

Therefore, I recommended that you make sure that your child is indeed developed in these four areas and is showing the "potty readiness" signals before you proceed.

Last, but not least, make sure that your child is NOT in another period of transition — such as the birth of a new sibling; recently moved into a new home, started daycare, or any other disruptive events. Toddlers like routine, and any changes are likely to cause setbacks in their behavior. Instead, wait until things have settled down and then start.

1. Physiological Development Readiness (Bladder and Bowel Control):

In order for your child to be able to eliminate when she wants to (voluntary vs. involuntary), her sphincter muscles have to have matured/developed enough to delay excretion for a brief period of time. All of my research, including that of the American Academy of Pediatrics, say that children's elimination muscles reach full maturity somewhere between 12-24 months, and the average age of maturity is 18 months.

How do you know if your child's elimination muscles are mature? Your child's behavior and actions will guide you in knowing how your child is developing in this area. Around her first birthday, your child will begin to recognize the sensation of a full rectum or bladder, signaling the need to eliminate. You observe this awareness through her behavior of squatting and grunting when having a bowel movement (BM) and tugging at the diaper when urinating.

At this age, she may not be able to delay elimination, but she needs to make the connection between the feeling of fullness and the act of excretion or urination. On the average, at about 18 months, your child's sphincter muscles mature and now your child has the ability to delay excretion for a brief period of time. You will notice that your child will no longer have bowel movements at night. Then you will observe that your child can stay dry for a few hours at a time. She will wake up dry from long naps, followed by waking up dry in the morning. She may urinate a lot at one time instead of a little throughout the day and there is some regularity of bowel movements.

Night time bowel control is usually achieved first, followed by day time bowel and bladder control and finally nighttime bladder control. So, if you think your child has full bladder and bowel control, should you start potty training? Not necessarily. Just because a child is physiologically ready to be potty trained does not mean that she has the other skills - motor, cognitive and verbal, emotional and social skills required for the whole potty training process.

Let's examine each of these skills:

2. Motor Skills Development Readiness

On the average, children will walk around the age of 12 months. Once your child has mastered walking and running, then she may be interested in acquiring other "grown up" skills and will start developing the gross and fine motor skills required for potty training. The main motor skill required is having sufficient finger and hand coordination skills to dress and undress, and more specifically to pull her underpants down and up.

3. Cognitive and Verbal Skills Readiness

The overall potty training process requires a complex combination of physical and cognitive tasks. Your child has to learn and become familiar with her body and its functions, associate the physical sensation with the proper response, visualize what she wants to do, create a plan to get to the potty, get there, remove the underwear and then begin to use the potty. Afterward, she must remain there long enough to finish, which requires memory and concentration.

As you teach your child all of these steps, she must have the ability to understand your explanations, commands and responses and to be able to put them all together to execute the entire potty training process. When you examine the process at this detailed level, you can understand why your child must have these cognitive and verbal skills in place to be able to successfully learn what is required.

It begins with body awareness and the ability to associate a feeling of fullness with the result — i.e. a BM or urination. This association is not made automatically. You need to reinforce this association by telling her what is happening, based on your observations.

At around the age of 2, children become aware of their body parts and it is your role to teach your child the words for the body parts. Use words that are comfortable to you and your family. This is also your opportunity to teach her all the other words that will be required in the potty training process.

The next steps in the potty training process require your child to have the capacity for symbolic thought, planning or problem solving and memory. She has to be taught that when she has the urge to go potty, that she should find her way to the potty, remove her clothing and then eliminate in the potty. She must have the ability for complex thinking and have the ability to extrapolate and problem solve. She needs to be able to stop doing whatever she is doing when she feels a sensation of fullness, figure out where the potty is, and find her way to it.

4. Emotional Growth and Social Awareness Readiness

This is probably the hardest readiness to gauge, especially since children go through several phases. The components that will help in determining your child's emotional and social readiness are self-mastery, desire for approval, and social awareness. The desire to master one's own body and environment is a powerful desire common to all toddlers and preschoolers. You will hear toddlers say "I can do it" and "I am a big girl now" — indications of the desire towards independence.

Sometimes, the need to control one's own body and environment are manifested in undesirable ways such as hiding when she has the urge to have a BM; having an accident for the sheer satisfaction of making the decision on where to go potty; or withholding stool and becoming constipated. When your child is in this phase of self-mastery, back off and try again later when she has moved into the more positive phase of self-mastery. Parents often underestimate the power of a child's desire for parental approval. As an adult, think about how you feel about your parents. Do you still care about what they think about you? Do you still want them to be proud of you? Most children have this desire, except for normal spurts of rebellion that occur throughout childhood. This desire to please a parent and receive parental praise and approval is a great tool that can assist in the process of potty training.

Social awareness is the ability to observe others coupled with the desire to be like them. At the age of 18 months, children become fascinated by the behavior of other children their own age or older. This is why often the 2nd and 3rd child is potty trained a lot earlier than the first child. By the age of 24-30 months, they start to understand gender differences and focus on imitating the behavior of the same sex parent.

Readiness Signals Summarized

The potty training readiness signals are summarized below by the four developmental areas, so that you can evaluate if your child is indeed ready to be potty trained.

1. Physiological readiness (Bladder & Bowel Control):

- Is your child aware of the elimination process? Does your child realize that she is about to go potty based on gestures? And do you recognize these gestures — i.e., posture, facial expressions, verbal cues?

- Has your child stopped having BM's through the night?
- Does your child urinate a lot at one time (vs. a little throughout the day)?
- Does your child remain dry for at least a few hours at a time?
- Does your child wake up (from a nap or from night sleep) with a dry diaper?
- Does your child have regular bowel movements? Children often have a bowel movement about half an hour after a meal.

2. Motor Skills/Physical Readiness:

- Has your child mastered walking and running?
- Does your child have enough finger and hand coordination skills to be able to dress and undress? More specifically, can your child pull her pants up and down?
- Does your child have the coordination and mastery of the mechanics required for toilet training?

3. Verbal & Cognitive Skills/Mental Readiness:

- Can your child follow your instructions? From simple instructions such as "show me your nose," to more complex instructions such as putting toys and other articles where they belong? Does your child have the ability for symbolic thought, planning/problem solving and memory?
- Does your child understand the vocabulary involved with toilet training? (Words such as poo, pee, potty, dry, wet,

diaper, big boy/girl pants etc. or whatever words work best for you and your family.)

- Is your child able to imitate behavior? Observe your child when she is playing – does your child imitate your behavior with her favorite toy – such as talking to a teddy bear?

4. Emotional Growth and Social Awareness Readiness:

- Does your child say "I can do it" or "I am a big boy/girl now?"
- Does your child look for or desire your approval?
- Does your child desire to be like others? Does she imitate behavior?

If you answered yes to all of the above questions, then your child is ready to begin toilet training. If you answered no to some of the questions, then give it some time, plus read the do's section included in this book for suggestions on helping your child get ready for potty training.

Are You Ready?

It is important that you as the parent or the person potty training get ready to potty train. Not only do you need to get all the tools and supplies together, you have to know and understand how to apply this method and be mentally ready for this task. Your mental readiness is a key component when it comes to potty training. It is easy to be upbeat and positive through the successes, however, your child will need you to remain calm, unemotional and positive when she is struggling and is having accidents. Therefore, taking some time to develop a plan and an understanding of what lies ahead will enable you to have realistic expectations for both you and your child.

Last but not least, think of this as another opportunity to create memories that you will treasure and remember for years to come. Also, you never know what this potty training adventure could lead to – for me, it led me to my third career eight years after I potty trained my boys!!

If you answered yes to all the questions listed above, then you are ready to potty train. If not, then read on.

1. Have you taught your child the appropriate vocabulary words for: *(Use words that are comfortable for you and your family to use.)*
   - Body parts? (e.g. penis, vagina, anus etc.)
   - Human waste / the elimination process? (e.g. poo, pee, wee, bowel movement etc.)
   - Sensory terms? (e.g. wet, dry etc)
   - Toileting equipment? (e.g. potty, toilet, underwear etc.)

2. Do you have a good understanding of how your child's development will affect his ability to learn?

3. Do you know your child's urination and BM schedule? *(Go to www.Potty-Training-in-One-Day.com to print out charts to record her schedule before you start potty training.)*

4. Do you have a clear understanding of the potty training in one day process?

5. Do you know your child's currency and have a plan for consequences/rewards?

6. Are you comfortable with implementing consequences for undesired behaviors?

7. Have you given thought to how you will remain calm & positive through the training process? (This is especially important when your child has an accident right after he gets up from the potty – this will happen!!)

8. Do you have a clear understanding of your child's perspective when it comes to potty training i.e. the detailed steps she has to learn?

9. Do you have all the required equipment?

10. Have you set realistic expectations for your child and for yourself?

11. Do you have a plan for nap time & night time? How about for after the "Big Day?"

Some Do's And Don'ts Of Potty Training

Do:

1. Start talking with your child about potty training and preparing her for the transition.

2. Talk about growing up and becoming a big girl, wearing big girl underwear and using the toilet like Mom and Dad.

3. Encourage your child to dress and undress herself. You want her to have good hand and finger co-ordination skills to be able to pull down her underwear and pants.

4. Start teaching your child the potty/toilet-training vocabu-

lary – such as pee or urine, poop or BM. The words you choose to use should be the ones that you and your family are comfortable with.

5. Teach your child the difference between wet and dry. Allow your child to learn the difference by touching wet and dry items.

6. Allow your child to observe you and others in your family when using the toilet. Explain what you are doing and teach your child the vocabulary.

7. Encourage your toddler to listen to her body. Teach her to say "I am thirsty" or "I need to go poo poo." Or if you see your child having a BM in her diaper, explain what is happening by saying something like "You are poo pooing. When you push like that, you make poo poo."

8. Observe your child's potty habits — i.e. you want to figure out if your child has a schedule. A lot of children will urinate a few minutes after waking and will have a BM about 30 minutes after eating. This will help you with planning your timing for the "Big Day."

9. Figure out what your child's currency is and decide how you are going to reward your child. Rewards can be verbal praise, non-verbal gestures such as hugging and kissing, special treats such as food, drinks, stickers and toys, or praise and rewards from other relatives, friends or even favorite superheroes.

10. Experiment and learn to use *Potty Scotty*™ or *Potty Patty*® before the "Big Day."

Don'ts

1. Don't start to potty train too soon. Make sure your child is ready. Review the section in this book: "Is Your Child Ready to Potty Train?"

2. Don't begin the process if things are currently unsettled in your life and in your child's life. Toddlers like routine and structure. Stress and change could cause a setback in your child's behaviors.

3. Don't get angry or punish your child for not wanting to go potty. Going to the potty is desired behavior and should be rewarded with positive reinforcement such as verbal encouragement and praise.

4. Do not get angry if your child has an accident. Don't show disgust or punish your child. Instead, you should set the expectation that the logical consequence of this behavior is to practice running back and forth to the potty 10 times. Then, follow through with this consequence without showing any anger.

5. Don't pressure your child into potty training. You want your child to be excited and enthusiastic about potty training and to view the whole experience as growing up.

6. Don't be pressured into potty training by others close to you. Potty training cannot be and should not be rushed. Every child is different and both you and your child will know when it is the right time.

7. Don't have unrealistic expectations. Some children are very easy to train, while others are very challenging. Be

prepared by setting realistic expectations and be ready to clean up accidents.

8. Don't expect miracles. By this, I mean that you should not have unrealistic expectations of your child. Your child **will have** accidents and you **will have** to clean them up and do the follow-up practice. There is no miracle pill – it will take some work and perseverance to be successful.

Required Potty Training Equipment:

Potty Scotty™ or Potty Patty® Training Doll

These dolls are drink and wet-on-demand™ and hold water until you want them to go pee. They are dressed in a two- piece outfit, so that the top piece can be easily removed when potty training.

The dolls are also wearing a diaper under-

neath their clothes.

The dolls are named *Potty Scotty™* or *Potty Patty®*; however, if your child wants to call the doll by another name, let them rename the doll. The important thing is that your child identify with the doll. Calling the doll by a name helps with this identification process.

3 "big kid" underwear

Potty Scotty™ and Potty Patty® will change into the underwear on the "Big Day." The additional underwear is to change the doll when she has an accident on the "Big Day."

Bottles for the dolls to drink water

Potty Scotty™ and Potty Patty® should only be given water. Any other fluids will ruin the doll – including clear fluids such as apple juice.

Potty Scotty ™ and Potty Patty® dolls and their accessories conform to the safety requirements of ASTM F963 and EN91.

Potty Scotty™ or Potty Patty® Padded Training Pants for your child

I recommend that you have at least six pairs of padded potty training pants. Having more training pants on hand will reduce the need to do laundry right away. Twelve pairs would be great and 18 would be excellent. These training pants are designed to fit loosely so that they can be pulled on and off by the toddler without adult help. Not only does this increase the chance of getting to the potty on time, but it also makes the whole process much more independent, which is the goal of this potty

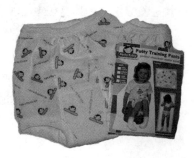

training program. When the training underwear are wet, they will make toddlers feel uncomfortable and therefore the toddlers will be more aware of their excretory functions, especially when compared to diapers and pull-ons. Check to make sure that the "big kid" underwear fit your child loosely and she will be able to pull them off easily.

The *Potty Scotty™ or Potty Patty®* Potty Chair

This simple basic one piece molded plastic potty is light, portable and easy to clean. Design features include a low splashguard; cut outs in the front and sides for easy lifting and is low-to-the-ground to encourage the more natural squatting position for toileting.

This basic potty is all that is required to potty train your child. If you already have another potty that your child is attached to, use it. Just try and use the same potty for the doll and for your child.

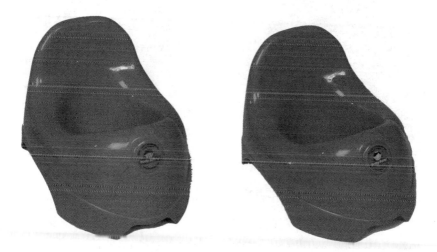

The *Potty Scotty™ or Potty Patty®* Toilet/Potty Seat

This toilet seat is made of durable recycled polypropylene and is designed not only for safety, but for comfort and fun. It is designed to fit any standard toilet. It is excellent for initial potty training and will help your child make the transition from the potty to the toilet. It is very portable and easy to move from toilet to toilet, since it is not permanently attached to the adult toilet. The non-slip rubber edges hold the potty seat in place. The potty seat has a hook to hang it up when not in use.

Favorite Beverages

You should have plenty of your child's favorite beverages in her favorite bottle or sippy cup on the day of the potty training. You may want a selection on hand, so that your child has a choice and is happy and willing to take in plenty of fluids.

Rewards - Salty and Sweet Treats

Have salty treats handy that your child likes, which will make her thirsty for some of the beverages. Sweet treats such as chocolate and candies that your child loves would be good to use as rewards for desired behavior.

CAUTION: If your child is prone to constipation, stay away from sodas if at all possible, especially those with caffeine. Limit the use of chocolate also. (See sections on Constipation and BM training)

Rewards

If you do not like the idea of food as a reward, you could use stickers or small toys. You could buy a number of small toys and have them in a basket, wrapped or unwrapped. One of the parents who used this program, used water toys with a bowl of lukewarm water. If your child has a full bladder and is sitting on the potty and plays with the toys in the lukewarm water, she is sure to urinate in the potty!!

Step Stool

Place a step stool in the bathroom so that your child can reach the sink to wash her hands.

Extra Towels and Cleaning Supplies

Have some extra towels and cleansers on hand to clean up the water and beverage spills, along with some stain and odor remover to clean up those accidents.

Flushable Wipes

You may want to consider getting flushable wipes as they may be more comfortable for your child's sensitive bottom.

Added Protection

Depending on your plan for nap and nighttime, you may want

to get a waterproof mattress pad and some overnight under-wear or waterproof covers or vinyl underpants to put over the "big kid" underwear.

Supplies needed after the "Big Day"

Life goes on and you will soon have to leave the house with your toddler before she is completely accident free. This is actually a good thing, because your toddler also has to learn how to manage going potty away from home.

Having some of these items ahead of time will make it pleasant for both you and your child.

1. Portable/Travel Potty Chair for the car.
2. Portable/Travel Potty Seat for placing on top of adult toilet seats.
3. Disposable potty seat liners for use in public restrooms.
4. Protection for your car seat.
5. Container with lots of extra clothes, underwear, socks and don't forget extra shoes.
6. Cleaning supplies to clean up the accident.
7. Supply of plastic bags to contain the wet clothes.

Visit www.Potty-Training-in-One-Day.com to see the list of recommended products.

Selecting The Big Day

The best time of year to potty train your child is spring and summer. The reason for this is that on the "Big Day" and for a few days following the "Big Day," you want to have your child wearing the minimal amount of clothing — i.e. basically a tee shirt and the "big kid" underwear. This enables your child to potty easily and independently, which will give her a huge sense of accomplishment.

The best day to potty train is probably a Thursday or Friday for most people. Ideally, you want to select a time when you can be home with your child for at least a three-day stretch. This allows both you and your child to focus on and complete the potty training process. It is easier for your child to master this skill if she has the opportunity to spend a quiet, relaxed weekend at home in her "big kid" underwear and tee shirt and be around her potty.

It is a lot easier on you, when you don't have to deal with accidents outside the home. Also, it is most important to select a day when you can devote 4-8 hours of focused one-on-one time with your toddler. On the "Big Day," you will want to eliminate all distractions — turn off all the gadgets such as the TVs, radios, phones, faxes, cell phones, pagers, etc. Make arrangements to take your other children to a sitter and ask the other adults in the house to leave, so that there is only your toddler and yourself.

Remove the toys and any other distractions from the potty training area. The goal is to create an environment where you and your toddler can spend focused quality time on the potty training activities. I recommend starting as soon after breakfast as possible. I also recommend having lunch and dinner preplanned, so that you do not have to take time away from potty training to prepare meals. Pick a day and mark your calendar. Show this to your child and start building up the excitement for this "Big Day."

Get all the supplies together. Be prepared mentally and physically to handle potty accidents and clean ups. Most children who are potty trained using this method will be accident free in one to two weeks.

Select an area in your home that is conducive to training. It should be an area where the floors can easily be cleaned. I trained my children in our kitchen. The linoleum floors made cleaning the water and beverage spills easier to deal with. It was adjacent to our family room and the bathroom. Remember, the potty will not reside in the kitchen forever – it is only for a very limited time.

Most people who choose to use the potty training in one day are surprised by how quickly their child learns to go potty and that the potty accidents are limited to a few days.

SECTION III

The Big Day

The anticipation is over. The "Big Day" is here. You and your child are both ready and excited that this day of giving up diapers forever is finally here. You have all the equipment you need and have created an environment where you and your child are going to spend some quality time together – it is time to get going.

Outlined below is a summary of the "ideal" Big Day.

1. You will switch from using diapers or pull-ons to using "big kid" underwear. Both your child and his *Potty Scotty*™ *or Patty Potty*® doll will give up their diapers forever and will change from diapers to "big kid" underwear.

2. With your assistance and guidance your child will teach his doll to use the potty. He will start by giving the doll water. You will give your child his favorite drink as well. Your child will then remove the doll's "big kid" underwear and make the doll pee on the potty.

3. You will both reward (in the manner chosen by you) the doll for being such a big boy. You and your child will make the doll feel special and grown up. Let your child know that he will also be rewarded when he urinates in the potty.

4. You will continue to give your child fluids and ask him to go pee in the potty. While waiting for your child to pee, make the doll have an accident. In a very positive way, you will teach your child the consequences of having an accident by making the doll practice going to the potty three times.

5. When your child has an accident, you will help him clean up and change.

6. Your child will practice going back and forth to the potty at least 10 times.

7. You will continue to ask your child to practice pulling his pants down and sitting on the potty. When your child pees in the potty, you will celebrate your child's success with the reward you had planned for him.

8. Congratulations! You and your child will have done it. No more diapers!

This is the ideal scenario. Every child is an individual, so the "Big Day" will play out differently for each parent and child. Therefore, I have broken down the "Big Day into **three major activities**:

1. The Growing Up Ceremony.
2. Learning "desired behaviors" and their consequences.
3. Learning "undesired behaviors" and their consequences.

Your goal is to get through all the three major activities and achieve the results identified. The order in which you will get through these activities will depend on what your child does.

Activity # 1:
The Growing Up Ceremony

Create a feeling for your child that he is growing up. This gives you an opportunity to set your child's expectations about "big kid" underwear and diapers.

1. Set out the snacks and drinks

2. Tell your child that both the doll and your child are going to change from diapers to their "big kid" underwear. You are verbalizing how this is such a great day; your child is a big boy and is giving up diapers forever.

3. Help and guide your child to change the doll's under-

wear and let your child change himself with as little assistance from you as is possible. After all, that is what will be required of your child, so be patient, guide verbally, but keep those hands to yourself!

4. Leave the trousers off for both the doll and your child. Hopefully, you can also remove your child's socks and shoes. Having only the underwear on makes it a lot easier for your child to pull his underwear on and off. It also makes cleaning up a lot easier when your child has an accident.

Activity #1: Expectations About Growing Up

Now, your child and the doll are wearing "big kid" underwear and your child is feeling all grown up. Your child also knows that he will not be wearing diapers or pull-ons anymore. From this day forward, he will be wearing "big kid" underwear.

Activity #2:
Learning Desired Behaviors And Consequences

You will teach your child what the desired behaviors are (i.e. pees and poos in the potty and to have dry pants) and communicate the consequences of these desired behaviors (rewards such as party, phone call or treats).Now that your child and the doll are in their training underwear, it is time to bring out the drinks. First offer your child his favorite beverage and then offer the doll his favorite beverage, which is water.

It is important that you are familiar with how *Potty Scotty*™ *and Patty Potty*® operate and how they drink water. It is key that you have spent some time familiarizing yourself with the doll. The risk of operating the doll for the first time on the "Big Day" is that things may not go smoothly and your child may lose the interest and the enthusiasm that you have built up in anticipation of this great day.

Now, guide your child to feed the doll. The doll needs to drink at least one full bottle in order for it to have a decent stream of "pee." Make sure that you already have some water in the doll beforehand, so if your child is impatient with feeding the doll, you can still make the doll go potty.

While you and your child are feeding the doll, you are also encouraging your child to drink his beverage.

A note from experience:

What should you do if your child has an accident at this point? My child had a BM in his training pants as we were getting started with the doll. The book I was using did not tell me what to do. I remember thinking – now what?

This is not in my plan and I am not prepared to handle this – what should I do? I actually flipped through the book looking to see if I could find the section on what to do when this happens. It did not exist. I put the book down and calmly led my child into the bathroom. We cleaned up the mess and got him into a fresh clean pair of underwear. I remained very calm and I did not have any positive or negative discussion with him – since we were only starting out. I just did what I had to do and we came back into the kitchen and continued on as if nothing had happened.

I would recommend that you do what I did. If your child has an accident while you are teaching him how to potty the doll, then there are no consequences for this undesired behavior. However, if an accident (either urination or BM) occurs after the expectations for the consequences have been taught, then you have to follow through on making your child practice going back and forth from the potty 10 times.

Back to our plan. After the doll has had a bottle, you will suggest to your child that the doll would like to go "pee pee." Help and guide your child to pull down the doll's pants, sit it on the potty and make it pee. This is the moment. You are thrilled. You might throw confetti or streamers and make a lot of noise for positive reinforcement. I used both verbal and non-verbal positive reinforcement and junk food – potato chips as a reward for the doll, which of course my child ended up eating.

I'd like to share my thoughts and observations on potty training boys – even though *Potty Scotty*™ can pee standing up or sitting down, I recommend sitting him down to pee. The main reason that you want to teach your boy child to urinate sitting down is that BM and urine tend to come out at the same time, so if you teach your child to urinate sitting down, then you can continue with the same process for bowel movements.

The next step is rewards — how you reward the doll and your child is up to you. The bottom line is that you want to use something that you know your child will respond to. What you are doing by rewarding the doll is setting the expectations with your child. Your child is smart enough to extrapolate that he will receive a reward when he meets the expectations. Dr. Phil's suggestion is tell your child that he can call his superhero when he pees in the potty. On Dr. Phil's show, the child called Thomas the Tank Engine.

I had told my child that we would call his Daddy, and how proud both Daddy and I would be. Daddy was expecting the call and knew what had to be done. We also had a certificate that Dad and I signed and put in a frame to show the other relatives. You select what you know will work for your child.

The other part about setting expectations goes with the behaviors you expect from your child after he has peed. The book I used suggested that the child be taught to empty the potty into the toilet and bring the potty back to the training area. I was not comfortable with my child carrying a potty full of urine, so I did it while he accompanied me to the bathroom. The book did not talk about washing hands, however, and this is something that is very important. So, after I emptied the potty, we all washed our hands —including the doll!

My recommendation is that you give some thought to the details of what happens after the doll and child pee in the potty and what you can and cannot live with. You decide what steps/ actions you expect your child to perform independently from the "Big Day." Then, based on what you can live with, decide what needs to be done after the doll has peed.

Okay, back to the doll and the doll's reward. After the doll had peed in the potty, I verbally praised the doll and encouraged my child to praise the doll along with me. After the doll has peed, has been rewarded, and the clean up has been completed, you should go back to the training area. Your child has seen a desired behavior and its consequence. You now want your child to demonstrate this behavior for you.

So prompt your child to use the potty. Use words like "It is your turn to use the potty" and guide your child towards the potty. Verbally guide your child to lower his pants and sit on the potty.

You want your child to sit on the potty for at least 5 minutes. You want your child to be relaxed enough to be able to urinate. If you have figured out your child's schedule, try and have your child on the potty at the time when he would normally go. If your child is content on sitting on the potty, let him sit. Sit beside him and provide positive verbal feedback. If your child does not want to sit any longer, verbally guide him to pull up his underwear. Make sure that you are providing plenty of verbal and non-verbal feedback for all the desired behaviors – i.e. pulling pants down, sitting on the potty, pulling pants up, washing hands etc.

The other desired behavior that you want your child to learn about is dry pants. We do this by focusing on desired behavior with the doll. You ask your child to inspect the dolls' underwear by touching them to make sure that they are dry. You ask him to praise the doll for having dry underwear, you verbalize how big kids pee and poo in the potty, and how you are very proud of *Potty Scotty*™ for keeping his underwear dry. Your child should reward the doll and then you will ask your child to inspect his own underwear by touching them to make sure that they are dry.

If they are dry, you will praise and reward your child.

Do the doll and child inspections at least two more times about 5 minutes apart, for a total of three dry pants inspections. Interspersed with dry pants inspections will be the prompted reminder practice sessions of lowering pants and sitting on the potty for at least 5 minutes at a time. You should also try and get in at least 3-5 of these prompted reminder practice sessions during the day. Hopefully, your child will urinate in the potty during one of these practice sessions.

Since every child is an individual, it is impossible to predict exactly how the day's events will unfold. In the next graphic, I charted the visual time line for the first two activities.

Visual Time Line for the "Big Day"

Activity 1: Celebrate Growing Up

Give Up Diapers → Set Expectations

Activity 2: Desired Behavior & Consequences

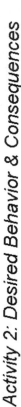
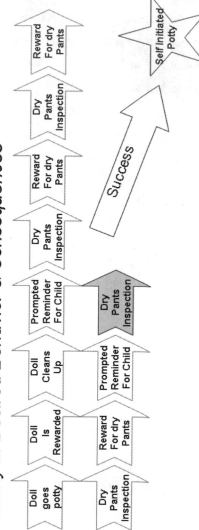

Doll goes potty → Doll Is Rewarded → Doll Cleans Up → Prompted Reminder For Child

Dry Pants Inspection → Reward For dry Pants → Prompted Reminder For Child → Dry Pants Inspection

Dry Pants Inspection → Reward For dry Pants → Dry Pants Inspection → Reward For dry Pants

Success → Self Initiated Potty

You can stop activity Number Two and move to activity Number Three when you are certain that your child understands that you desire dry underwear and you expect him to pee and poo in the potty.

Activity #2 Expectations for Desired Behaviors and Consequences

Your child understands that the desired behaviors are to pee and poo in the potty and have dry pants. These desired behaviors are rewarded with verbal and non-verbal praise, treats and maybe even a party or a call to a superhero.

Activity #3: *Learning Undesired Behaviors And Consequences*

You must teach your child what the undesired behaviors are (i.e. not peeing in the potty and wet pants) and to communicate the logical consequences of these undesired behaviors: clean up and practice.

Teach your child the undesired behavior and consequences by encouraging your child to drink more fluids. While your child is not looking, you wet the doll's underwear. On the next dry pants inspection, the doll's underwear is wet – this is the undesired behavior. So, now you verbalize and explain to your child how this is the undesired behavior. You could say something like "Big boys/girls do not wet their pants, they urinate and poo in the potty. And, when they do wet their pants, they have to practice going on the potty." Then have your child help the doll clean up and put on dry "big kid" pants. Then have your child make the doll practice going to the potty. Explain to your child that by practicing, the doll will learn that he has to pee in the potty.

Let your child help the doll to clean up and change his underwear. How much clean up your child does depends on what you have decided earlier. Then let your child take the doll from where the doll had the accident to the potty, help the doll pull her underwear down and sit on the potty. Your child will help the doll pull the underwear back up and walk the doll back to where the doll first had the accident.

Next, your child will practice this with the doll two more times, for a total of three full back and forth practice runs. You will help your child verbalize how he expects the doll to pee in the potty and how this practice will help the doll keep his underwear dry and help pee in the potty. You practice this with your child until you know that he understands the consequences of wet underwear.

As mentioned earlier, if your child has an accident before using the doll, assist with clean up and continue where you left off. Since this method first teaches the child about desired behaviors and their consequences and then about the undesired behaviors and their consequences, you have to judge where your child is in this process and then continue and finish teaching your child the rest of the process.

As you go along, you want to encourage your child to drink plenty of fluids. You will continue to do dry pants inspections, as well as prompted reminder practice sessions of sitting on the potty. Most children will urinate a number of times in one day and will urinate anywhere between half an hour to an hour after having a large drink. The next graphic provides a visual timeline for this activity.

If your child has not yet used the potty to urinate, it is a matter of waiting it out. If your child has had an accident, do the 10 practice runs back and forth to the potty (see follow-up section below for more details). When your child urinates in the potty, celebrate his success as you had planned with your child.

Congratulations, you and your child have done it. No more diapers. No more pull-ons. Just "big kid" underwear. A few more accident clean-ups and you are ready to move on to other parenting challenges!

Activity #3 Expectations Undesired Behaviors And Consequences

Your child helps *Potty Scotty*™ *or Potty Patty*® to change into dry underwear and has helped the doll practice going to the potty. Your child knows the consequences of undesired behaviors and should know that he will have the same consequences for these undesired behaviors.

Visual Time Line for the "Big Day"

Activity 3: Undesired Behavior & Consequences

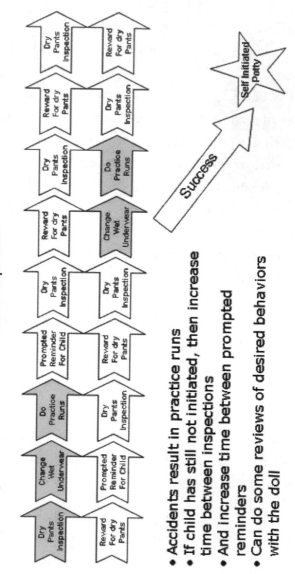

- Accidents result in practice runs
- If child has still not initiated, then increase time between inspections
- And increase time between prompted reminders
- Can do some reviews of desired behaviors with the doll

After Goal Achievement

Ideally, if your child is staying on plan, you should be about
2 – 4 hours into your "Big Day." You have celebrated his success with a great big celebration. There was a lot of excitement,
but hopefully, things are becoming calm again. You have also
had the opportunity to get through all the activities and you are
confident that your child knows the behavior expected and associated consequences.

Now it is time to switch your focus into <u>Maintenance Mode</u>.

You can continue to play with the doll if your child is still
interested in it or you can move on to other things. You want to
maintain the nice, cozy, warm atmosphere you have created with
your child and you want to continue spending one-on-one time
with your child. I recommend activities that will maintain this
atmosphere, such as reading or playing with toys. You do not
want to do anything too involved, because you do not want to
lose the focus and you do not want your child so involved in
something else that it would be hard to leave it to go use the
potty.

Now that your child knows that you desire him to pee on the
potty, you want your child to take the initiative to use the potty,
instead of being directed to use the potty. The goal is to have
your child use the potty when he needs to.

Increase the time in between dry pant inspections and instead of *directing* your child to use the potty, *suggest* that he use
the potty. Do not ask your toddler if he needs to use the potty –
since questions such as "Do you need to use the potty?" could

get a no response, especially if your toddler is in that negative-phase. You started the day with very directive statements, e.g. "Johnny, it's your turn to use the potty." As the day progresses, you want to move to more suggestive statements, e.g. "Johnny, you should use the potty" and by the end of the day, you want very general statements e.g. "Johnny, show me where you pee?" or "Johnny, do you have dry pants?"

Once your child has **initiated using the potty at least two times**, you are on the home stretch. You now have to manage the accidents and start working on including Bowel Movement training.

Ideally, you want to keep your child in just underwear for the next few days until he is fully potty trained, including having BMs in the potty. I know that this is not possible for all parents.

I was working outside the home at the time I potty trained my children. With my first child, I took him to the day care the next day. I took plenty of extra clothes, underwear and shoes and made sure that they did not put diapers on him during the day. He did have one accident at the day care. Our "Big Day" was a Thursday, he went to the day care on Friday and then he spent the weekend at home in underwear and a tee shirt. He had two accidents on Saturday, which was our hardest day, because we had to do the practice runs. After the second practice run on Saturday, my child decided it was easier to use the potty than do the practice runs with mom. He was fully potty trained.

Follow Up And Maintenance

When your child has an accident, you help her clean up and change clothing. Then you do the practice runs with your child. This is definitely the hardest part of the potty training process.

It is simple to get your child to go potty for the first few times because she knows there is a reward coming. However, your toddler may not fully comprehend that you expect her to do this all of the time – that you expect her to stop playing when she has to go to the bathroom. Up until now, she could go potty (in her diaper) and play at the same time.

Now, all of a sudden, you have changed the rules on her! You have told her, you have demonstrated this to your child with *Potty Scotty*™ *or Potty Patty*®, but not all children can quickly connect the dots. As a parent of a toddler, you have already learned that parenting is about setting boundaries or expectations and that there are consequences for not meeting the expectations.

The hardest part for most parents is to CONSISTENTLY follow through on the consequences. You know your child and you know that she will test the boundaries you have set for her. So, you will have to consistently follow through on consequences.

The logical consequences for having an accident are to practice expected behavior. This means taking her to the potty or bathroom 10 times in a row. This also helps in building your child's muscle memory.

Your child may have fun the first few times, but the novelty will quickly wear off. However, as a parent, the key is following through consistently. For my older son, the novelty of practice ended for him after the first five practice runs after his first accident.

I did not give in to him or his whining. I did not get angry (even though I was feeling it) or raise my voice, I was just very firm in my expectations of him and I was counting down the practices, so he would know that there was only 4, 3, 2, 1 more left. He did not like the second and third practice sessions at all, but again, I stood firm and after the fourth accident and practice session, he decided it was easier to use the potty to start with, than to have to run back and forth ten times from the bathroom.

Children will do less desirable things to access more desirable things. My son decided that taking time away from play to go potty was much better than having to do those darn practice runs. When your child has an accident, do not get angry or show disgust. Do verbalize the fact that you expect her to use the potty e.g. "Big girls do not wet their pants, they pee/poo in the potty." Once is enough for most children.

Help your child clean up and change into clean underwear. Then, help your child practice going to the potty 10 times. You will remind your child *Potty Patty*® had to practice going after she wet her pants. "Jane has to practice going to the potty, too."

Try and get it done as quickly as possible. Physically guide your child to the potty, have her lower her underwear, sit on the potty for only a second, get up, pull up the pants. Run to another part of the house.

Say something like "What would Jane do if she was in the playroom playing and she had to pee? Jane would run to the potty to pee." Run back to the potty with your child and repeat this eight more times.

If your child starts to get tired, start counting down, but do get those 10 runs in. I did all 10 runs with my children, and this is the hardest part of the whole process. You have to decide whether cleaning up after a few accidents, plus consistently making your child practice going to the potty is worth having a child that is fully potty trained in less than two weeks.

Toileting is a developmental skill similar to walking or running and it takes some time to master. Some toddlers get up and start walking without ever looking back, yet others will have many falls before they get there. Potty training is the same. Your toddler may have zero accidents or he may have quite a few before he is fully trained. You have to commit to helping him learn as many times as he may need. It is up to you!

Should You Ever Use Pull-Ons During The Day?

The answer is very simple – no. Pull-ons are disposable diapers disguised as underwear. The wonderful part about today's diapers and pull-ons is that they are designed to keep the wetness away from the child. Your child will have a very different experience when he goes potty in the "big kid" underwear compared to the diaper or pull-on. The "big kid" underwear is designed NOT to contain the mess and not to keep the wetness away from your child. This unpleasantness is meant to be a motivator to use the potty. I know that this means more work for you and it is not as convenient, however, it is part of the process and using pull-ons *will* have a negative impact in the overall success of this method.

What About Naptime?

If your child is still taking naps, then plan your "Big Day" around this nap. If possible, try and start at least four hours before naptime. If you have not completed the potty training by naptime, then let your child take a nap. Working with a cranky child is not worth the trouble. I would recommend putting a mattress pad on top of the sheets or a plastic liner and absorbent towels between the sheets and the mattress and let your child nap in the "big kid" training underwear. You should not use diapers or pull-ons. When your child wakes up, continue potty training where you had left off.

Night Time Potty Training

Night-time potty training means the same as day time potty training — when your child has the urge to urinate, he should go to the potty to urinate. However, achieving night time control is not simply a learned skill, but rather a physiological development and the control is largely involuntary. In some cases, circumstances require learning how to achieve night time control (see bed wetting section).

Babies urinate around the clock, and then at about the average age age of 18 months, as the sphincter muscles mature, toddlers will make the transition from urinating around the clock to only urinating during the waking hours, as is the case with most adults. Make sure that your child's environment is set up so that she can get up and go use the potty or toilet if she has to. She has to be able to get out of her bed safely and easily. If you are comfortable with her going potty independently at night, then she should have easy access to the potty. If not, she should be able to come and get you, so that you can assist her with going to the potty or toilet.

On the following page is a table that shows the age at which children achieve night time control.

Age Of Child	% of Children Have Achieved Night Time Control
Under 3 years old.	66%.
Under 4 years old.	75%
Under 5 years old.	80%
Under 6 years old.	85%

The key to dealing with night time accidents is slightly different from dealing with day time accidents, because night time accidents are NOT voluntary. Your child does not have the ability to control the accident, so, there are no consequences given. As you face another clean up, realize that this is hard on your child as well. She does not want to have accidents any more than you do. The situation has to be very neutral. Just clean up and move on.

However, if your child is having more than two or three accidents per week, I would recommend using disposable pull-on diapers and making it less stressful on everyone involved. Monitor the situation and try to switch to cloth underwear when your child is a little older and may have achieved night time control. If your child is wetting at night and is trained during the day, consult with the child's pediatrician, especially if the child is five years old or older. Your overall plan for potty training should include a plan for night time potty training. How you address night time potty training is very much dependent on you and your child. My recommendations on how to approach night time potty training are:

1. If your child is dry most mornings, then definitely try moving to underwear and see if your child will actually stay dry and/or wake up to use the potty. Make sure that you have some mattress protection in place, so the clean-up can be done easily with minimal frustration. I really like the mattress pads that you can put on top of the bed sheets and wrap around both sides of the mattress. Have at least two of these on hand, so if and when you have to deal with an accident at night, you do not have to strip the whole bed, but rather just change the mattress pad.

2. If your child is waking up wet, then I recommend considering other options. Again, how you approach this depends on how often your child is wetting and your own tolerance level to accidents and accident clean up.

3. If your child is wetting often — two or three times per week — I recommend staying with disposable pull-on diapers. This makes it easier on every one involved. My only caution to the usage of disposable products is the issue of confusion in the child's mind, because the disposables do not let the child feel the wetness.

If you are going to use the disposable products, I would recommend the following:

- Tell your child that the pull-on diaper is night time pants for big kids. You want your child to be proud of the fact that she is now wearing big kids underwear and not diapers. If you have been using pull-on diapers already – switch to a different brand – so that your child will indeed see a difference.

- Put on the pull-on diaper just before bedtime. Have your child use the potty or toilet before bed, and then put on the pull-on diaper.

- Remove the pull-on diaper as soon as your child wakes up. Most people will urinate right after waking up. Give your child the opportunity to urinate in the potty or toilet instead of into the pull-on diaper.

4. If your child is wetting only occasionally, two or three times per month, you may want to use night time cloth training pants. There are a number of different brands available and many styles are available online. For a list of recommend products, visit my website at www.Potty-Training-in-One-Day.com. If your child is wetting only one or two times every three months – I recommend switching completely to regular underwear and using a good mattress pad until she is completely dry.

The bottom line is that just over half of children (66 percent) will be dry at night by the age of 3; however 33 percent of children, or one in every three children, will still wet at night while potty trained for day time. To be successful with night time potty training, do the following:

- Know your and your spouse's bed wetting history.
- Know your child's behavior pattern for waking up dry.
- Based on this information, be prepared with a plan on how you will address night time potty training.
- Be patient and be flexible; adjust your plan as needed.
- Consult your child's pediatrician if you have issues or concerns.

Leaving The House – Back To Normal Life

Eventually, you have to leave the house and get back into a normal routine. Once your child has initiated going potty at least five times, you know that she has connected all the dots and knows what is expected of her, you can leave the safety of your home and venture out into the real world with your child.

As I recommend in the preparation phase, this is one of the things you need to plan ahead of time, so that when the day arrives, you are ready. The most important thing you have to consider is what your child is going to be wearing when you head out the door. With my child, I stayed with the potty training underwear. I would recommend cloth training pants and if you are really worried about accidents and clean up, then consider some sort of waterproof cloth training pants or waterproof covers that go over the training pant to help reduce the mess. I do not recommend using diapers or pull-ons because those are behind you now and since your child will not feel the wetness in them, it will only cause confusion.

The next thing to consider is how you are going to clean up the accident. Chances are that your child will have an accident when you are out and you will have to clean it up, so why not be prepared for the worst. So, pack some items to take along with you; besides change of underwear and clothing, I recommend that you also take along socks and shoes, wipes and towels to help clean up, some cleaning solution to help clean up the mess and lots of plastic bags to contain the wet mess.

There are many products available on the market today that will ease the whole change and clean up process. Go to www.Potty-Training-in-One-Day.com for a list of recommended products.

The next thing to consider is where your child is going to go potty when you are out and about. Each child is an individual and each family will handle this differently. Think about how you would like to handle this and plan for it. You may want to have a travel potty chair on hand that your child will use, or you may want to have a travel potty seat that you will place on top of a public toilet seat that your child will use, or use potty seat covers on a public restroom toilet.

Again, there are many choices available. So, decide how you would like to handle this and be ready. Then communicate with your child on what you expect from her as you go out. Let your child know if you are planning on using a travel potty or a public restroom.

Let your child know that she has to let you know as soon as she feels the need to go potty. You will then quickly enable your child access to whatever means of potty you have decided to use. Some children will adapt to using public facilities without missing a beat, while others will take a few weeks or months before they are totally comfortable. You know your child best, so work with your child to let him know that he can also go potty away from home and do so very comfortably.

Fear Of Public Restrooms

This kind of fear might result from a child being afraid of the big toilet seat. I would recommend trying to find out from the child what she does not like about public restrooms, and then figure out how to work with her fear. If she is afraid of the big toilet – consider carrying a reducer. Many portable folding seats are available on the market. Or consider carrying a por table potty chair that she can use until she is comfortable with the big toilet seat.

Potty Training Resistance

When a child resists going potty, there is usually a good reason. Your job as a parent and coach is to play detective and find out why. Here are some general ideas that may help you figure out why your child might be resisting going to the potty independently. Address your child's concerns and you will have a much more cooperative child and things should go a lot smoother.

Confusion

Your child may be confused about the toilet training process or about what is expected from him. Since she does not understand you, she does not want to try, and will therefore resist. Confusion around expectations occur when the child is getting mixed messages from the parent. Consistency is the key. Create reasonable expectations according to your child's abilities, then express them clearly and frequently and follow through on what you say. Also, see section on BM Training and BM Resistance.

A painful BM

Constipation might be the cause of resistance to going to the potty. Observe your child's behavior and if you see any signs of skin irritation or a urinary tract infection, consult with your child's pediatrician.

Curiosity

Children are curious about what will happen if they resist their parents. A toddler could be testing the waters to see what will happen, simply to solicit a reaction. This gives them information on how far they can push you and when or where the boundaries are enforced.

Anxiety

Fear about the process of elimination, or fear of the potty

or the toilet, could be a cause of resistance. A child could develop fear or anxiety about the process of elimination if for some reason the experience has been negative in the past. This could come from experiencing pain while urinating due to a skin irritation or a painful BM, or a negative experience with a potty or a toilet seat.

Independence

Control issues might make it hard for him to satisfy your wishes at this time. One of the child development stages that a toddler goes through is the desire to master one's own body and environment. You will hear toddlers say "I can do it" and "I am a big boy/girl now" — indications of the desire towards independence.

So, if your toddler happens to be in this stage, she may not want to satisfy your wishes at this time and will want to demonstrate to you that indeed she is an independent human being and in control of herself!

Too much pressure to perform

A parent who constantly asks the toddler is she needs to go potty may spark resistance in the toddler, especially if she happens to be in an independent phase.

Inappropriate potty training

A toilet training technique that does not suit the child's personality or learning style could cause resistance. For example if you select the "Practice Makes Perfect method," where you have defined a potty schedule for your child who is extremely inde pendent and a self starter, you may find yourself in a power struggle. If you have a child that tends to day dream and is easily distracted, she may need you to set up a schedule and remind her to go and use the potty.

Other examples include - asking a shy child to use the potty in the kitchen or family room - around a lot of people. Shutting the bathroom door on a sociable toddler is not a good thing to do. Asking a physically active child to sit on the potty for more than 3-5 minutes at a time brings on stress.

Key Issues For Potty Training In One Day

Child Has Not Initiated Potty Training

The goal of the potty training in one day method is for your child to potty and/or toilet independently. To say it another way – your child will use the potty when he needs to and NOT when he is prompted by you.

When your child initiates going to the potty himself, you know that he completely understands and has connected the dots in his head. He knows and acknowledges that he has the urge to go, he has to hold it long enough to get to the potty, remove his underwear, sit on the potty and then he has to relax to let the elimination begin. There are a couple of possible reasons if by the end of the "Big Day" your child has not initiated going to the potty by himself.

1. The child has not had an opportunity to initiate going potty.

It is possible that as your day progressed there was not enough time in between your prompted reminders to allow your child to fill his bladder. He needs to experience the whole process of feeling fullness, the urge to go, and actually going. Make sure that you are allowing enough time between your prompted reminders. Increase the time to allow your child to go through the entire experience.

2. The child has not connected all the dots — i.e. he does not fully understand what he is required to do.

If your child has not connected all the dots, then your job as the coach and parent is to first figure out which one of the points he is having trouble with, then try teaching that part to your child again. If he is still not getting it, you may have to get creative and come up with a different way of teaching your child. This part can be difficult, especially if you get emotional and lose your objectivity. You are the adult in this situation and thus if something is not working, it is up to you to remain objective and to work out a solution.

Perhaps, your child is too young and not verbal enough to tell you that he does not understand what you want him to do. His actions speak louder than words and you need to objectively look at those actions and figure out what he is saying. Children want to go on the potty and be like their parents and/or their siblings. They truly want to do what pleases their parents. But when they don't know or don't quite understand what their parents want them to do, they don't have the ability to articulate and communicate that to you in words. Their actions and/or behavior will communicate to you, if you are effective in teaching him what he needs to learn.

To give you an example, I will share with you the story of what happened when I potty trained my friend's son, Gabe. We started after breakfast at about 9 am. We went through the various activities and Gabe seemed to grasp the concepts, but kept having accidents. It was about 12:30p.m. when he had his 5th accident of the day and I observed that he was not able to control the urge to go. I could see that he was starting to realize the feeling of fullness, but by the time he acknowledged it, it was usually too late.

So, we broke for lunch and I decided that we would stay in the kitchen and remain as close to the potty as possible and we would decrease the time between the prompted reminders (we were doing about 40 minutes between the prompted reminders at this point). After lunch, I prompted him to try and use the potty, but no luck. Then 15 minutes after lunch, came the second reminder. He sat on the potty again, but no luck. We remained in the kitchen and within 5-7 minutes of the second reminder, he initiated and successfully used the potty. We had our potty party!

Adjusting and shortening the time enabled him to mentally and physically practice the going potty behavior a couple of times before the urge and when the urge came, we were right there. So, if you think that your child has not connected all the dots required for him to initiate going potty, figure out where the gaps are and adjust accordingly. If you are at a loss, start the process of teaching him the desired behaviors again and then move on to undesired behaviors. Adjust your time between the prompted reminders and switch to less directive and more suggestive language for using the potty i.e instead of asking your child if he has to use the potty, ask him where he would go potty if he had to.

Why Do Practice Runs?

The goal of practice runs is to provide a consequence that your child will not like. This consequence builds muscle memory. After you clean up — i.e. him into clean underwear — you make him run to the potty from different parts of the house to simulate what he would do if he had to go potty. Do the first couple of runs from where he had the accident, but then move to different parts of the house - i.e. if Scotty was watching TV and had to potty what would he do?

He would run to the potty, pull his pants down and go potty. Basically running to the potty, pulling pants down, sitting on the potty, and then getting up and pulling the pants back up takes only a few seconds. Ten practice runs would take less than five minutes if your child is cooperative. If your child is having a tantrum, let him finish the tantrum, and then continue with the practice runs as if nothing had happened.

What If Your Child Urinates In The Potty While Doing Practice Runs?

If your child ends up urinating in the potty while doing the practice runs, then that should be cause for celebration. He demonstrated the desired behavior and should be rewarded for it and you can stop doing the practice runs.

The little ones are very smart – I had a mom call me and tell me that she rewarded her little one with an M&M for a small trickle during the practice runs and the next thing she knew – bed time took two hours – because her little one stretched it out by urinating and emptying the potty a little bit at a time to get those M&Ms.

You want the desired behavior and you want to reward it, however if your child is trying to manipulate the situation, make a correction. The next day, this Mom told her smart angel that they would empty the potty when it had a certain amount of pee in it and that is when he would get the M&Ms.

What If Practice Runs Are Not A Deterrent?

For some children, the 10 practice runs are not a deterrent – these children actually enjoy the activity. They think of it as a game and have fun doing it. If this is the case with your child, you need to find some other form of consequence that will not be fun and will be a true deterrent.

What If Your Child Gets Jealous Of The Doll?

This is not something that I have experienced first hand nor have I seen it mentioned in any of the research I have done on potty training. However, over the last two years, I have had a couple of mothers contact me and tell me that their children were getting jealous of the doll.

Here's a quotation from one mother:

When my son went on the potty the first time he didn't want Scotty at his party. He pulled Scotty off the table threw him behind the couch and replaced him with another stuffed animal.

This boy was feeling frustrated and he was frustrated because he was unable to meet parental expectations, but *Potty Scotty*™ was able to. So the child vented his frustration/anger on the doll. As a parent, you should know that your child wants to please you – so if you want your child to go the potty – your child wants to do that to please you.

But as you already know, learning to go potty is not a simple thing for children; Your child cannot simply go potty because he observed *Potty Scotty*™ going potty. Your child has to figure out a number of little steps and put them all together in perfect synchronicity to be able to go potty. He has to acknowledge the feeling of fullness and then hold back, get to the potty, remove their clothing, sit on the potty and then relax his sphincter muscles to enable elimination. Each child is an individual and some chil-

70

dren figure this out right away, while other take a while. And if your child has the personality of being hard on himself, he is getting frustrated with himself, because he cannot figure it out, and then he senses his parent getting frustrated with him – so that makes him feel worse about the fact that he is struggling.

Your child wants to do what you are asking, but has not connected all the dots and is therefore unable to meet your expectations. The doll on the other hand has no trouble meeting your expectations, so the child may not like the doll because the doll is able to meet parental expectations, while the child is unable to.

So, be gentle with your child as he learns how to use the potty. Try to remain objective, remind yourself that your child really does want to please you and as the adult it is your job to guide and coach your child in the areas where he needs help. Don't compare your child with *Potty Scotty*™ or *Potty Patty*® or with another child or sibling. Your child is an individual and will learn at his own pace. Focus on teaching.

Bowel Movement Training

In most children, bowel control develops before urinary control. Many toddlers will let you know that they are having a BM by their posture, gestures or facial expressions, but very few will let you know that they are urinating. So, if your child has bladder control, chances are excellent that he has bowel control. In most cases, bowel movement training will almost happen naturally. This means that BM's usually follow urination, so once children are trained to urinate in a potty chair or on the toilet, they will also have a BM while urinating.

You, as the parent have already set expectations that both pee pee and poo poo go into the potty, so that your child already knows what you expect. You, of course, will give your child the extra praise the first time your child has a BM in the potty, and in most cases, BM training flows naturally after urine training. This is exactly what happened with my children. They had a BM while urinating in the potty and of course got plenty of verbal and non verbal praise, which reassured them that this was the expected behavior. Both of my children did have a couple of small twists on BM training that I think are worth mentioning.

My headstrong older son had his first accident, which was a BM just as we were getting started on the "Big Day." So, during the potty training session, I used both terms when I verbalized desired behaviors — "Big boys pee and poo in the potty."

My organized methodical younger son had zero accidents; however, he did have to learn a couple of things about his own body. On the second and third night after his "Big Day", he woke me up to go use the potty, but when he sat on the potty, all he did was pass gas. It took him a number of times of sitting on the potty to pass gas, before he had learned the difference between passing gas and having a BM!!

Your Child's BM Schedule

I recommend that you know your child's BM schedule before you start potty training. Most toddlers do go at specific times in the day and many will go anywhere from 5-30 minutes after a meal, especially breakfast. When the stomach is full, the colon is often stimulated to empty. I did not know that this was something I should have known before I started potty training my older son. We got started with potty training right after breakfast and sure enough, about 10 -15 minutes into the training, he had a BM.

I did not know what to do and so I distinctly remember flipping through the book I used to see what I should do. BM training was not really addressed in this book, so I cleaned him up and went on with the training as if nothing had happened. This was the right thing to do.

However, had I been aware of this timing, I would have waited for him to have the BM before we got started with potty training.

Knowing your toddler's BM schedule can be a help in a number of ways.

1. If you know her schedule, you can schedule your potty training accordingly.
2. You can encourage your toddler to sit on the potty at that time with the hope that she has a BM in the potty. This will get both of you off to a great start.
3. Knowing your child's schedule and routine equips you with better information, so that you are better able to know if your child's BM routine changes because of potty training or illness.
4. It will enable you to help avoid constipation issues. (See section on constipation).

Go to www.Potty-Training-In-One-Day.com to print out a Bowel Movement Chart.

Change In BM Schedule

Children are little people, and just as with adults, when we experience a change in our daily routine, such as a vacation or a business trip, we may not have a BM for a couple of days.

Children who are being potty trained and experience the change from diapers to training pants may also not have a BM for a couple of days. This is normal and what you want to do as a parent is to make sure you are fully aware of this and are monitoring your child's BMs.

Give your child plenty of fluids, because fluids keep the stool soft. Apple juice and prune juice are good for softening the stool. Stay away from sodas, especially ones with caffeine, as these tend to dry out the system. Chocolate also has caffeine, so if you are using chocolates as a reward, be careful with the amount of chocolate your child is consuming.

Food also has an impact, so try and stay away from foods made with white flour, bananas, rice and soy. Fruits and vegetables are good choices – such as plums, peaches, apricots, pears, peas, carrots, broccoli, cauliflower etc. and of course raisins, prunes and dried fruits.

You do not want the stool to get hard, because if the stool becomes hard, it is more difficult to pass it and could cause discomfort. A child who experiences a painful BM may become resistant to having BMs in the potty (see section on BM resistance). Once your child is comfortable with his new routine of potty training, bowel movements will follow and a new routine with urinations and BMs in the potty will be established.

Constipation

According to the American Academy of Pediatrics, a typical child should have the following BMs per day and week.

Child's Age	Avg BMs/	# of BMS/ Wk
1-3 Yrs.	1.4	4-21
Over 3 Years	1	3-14

Constipation refers to infrequent (less than 3 BMs per week) or incomplete bowel movements. The term is also used to refer to stools that are hard or difficult to pass.

Bear in mind, the consistency and frequency of stools change day to day as these are directly dependent on what we eat.

How Do You Know If Your Child Is Constipated?

Because each child is different and hardness is a relative term, the easiest way to know if your child is constipated is to look for the following symptoms:

- Hc has fewer than three bowel movements a week.
- The stools are hard, dry and unusually large.

- The stools are difficult to pass.
- Your child seems to be straining hard to have a bowel movement.
- Hiding to have a bowel movement.
- Grunting and squatting to help move the stool out of his system.
- If having a bowel movement is painful – suspect this if your child seems to be trying to hold the bowel in (e.g. by crossing the legs or sitting up on the heels) or if your child seems frightened of using the toilet.
- Passing an excessive amount of gas or belching frequently.
- Leakage of small amounts of soft stool resembling diarrhea.
- More frequent urination because of pressure on the bladder.

To be certain about whether your child is constipated or not, it is best to consult with your pediatrician.

How Does Constipation Get Started?

Constipation can result after a major event or a significant change in a child's life such as:

1. Potty training
2. Illness or medications
3. Some stressful event
4. Change in routine or diet

5. Unavailability of toilets

6. Because a child is too busy playing

When a child gets constipated, she may experience a painful BM. The next time she has an urge to have a BM, the memory of the painful negative experience will cause her to hold back. When she decides to hold back on the urge to have a BM, the stool sits in the colon. When stool sits in the colon, the water in the stool is reabsorbed back by the body and the stool tends to become hard. When the stool becomes hard, it can be very painful to pass. So, when the child decides to go ahead and have the BM, or can no longer hold it, the BM ends up painful, thus reinforcing the negative experience.

Therefore, the next time the child has to urge to have a BM, she withholds, and the cycle starts again, leading to constipation and other problems related to resistance to BM training, soiling or encopresis and even potentially bed wetting.

Soiling Or Encopresis

Soiling or Encopresis is the term used for lack of control of bowel movements for **anyone over the age of four**. The leakage may occur during the day or night. It is fairly common; 1-3 percent of children over the age of four are known to have encopresis and it is more common in boys than it is in girls.

Alternate terms used to describe these behaviors are soiling, fecal soiling, fecal incontinence, bowel movement withholding, bowel movement resistance, stool toileting refusal (STR); the medical term being encopresis.

There are two types of encropesis:

1. Retentive Encopresis.
2. Nonretentive Encopresis (also called BM Resistance)

1. Retentive Encopresis

About 80 to 95 percent of all cases are retentive encopresis. Children with this disorder have an **underlying medical reason for soiling**. Retentive encopresis is most often the result of chronic **constipation** and fecal impaction. In these children, feces have become impacted in the child's colon, causing it to distend. This causes the child to not feel the urge to defecate.

The anal sphincter muscle becomes weak and unable to contain the soft stools that pass around the impaction. Despite the constipation, these children actually do have regular, though soft, bowel movements that they are unable to control. The child may not even be aware that he or she has defecated until the fecal matter has already passed. Many children have a history of constipation that extends back as far as five years before the problem is brought to medical attention.

2. Non Retentive Encopresis (also called BM Resistance)

The remaining cases have no physical condition that bars normal toileting behaviors. This type, **non retentive encopre-**

sis, is a behavioral condition in which the child refuses to defecate in a toilet. The children will urinate in the potty or toilet, but will refuse to poop in the potty or the toilet. The children will either soil their underwear, or will wait until they are in a diaper or pull-ons to have the BM. Some will wait until naptime or bedtime to have the BM. Yet, other children will simply refuse to poop at all and end up with chronic constipation. The bottom line is that these children resist having a BM in the toilet and will find ways and tactics to avoid using the toilet.

Non retentive encopresis also called functional encopresis, bowel movement resistance, bowel movement withholding or even stool toileting refusal (STR).

Dr. Bruce Taubman at the University Of Pennsylvania School Of Medicine has conducted a number of studies on toilet training and more specifically on bowel movement resistance/withholding or stool toileting refusal (STR) is what he calls it. In one of his studies, he found that stool toileting refusal is common; one in five children in his study population refused to use the potty for BMs and 85% of the STRs wore underwear, but asked for a diaper or pull-on to eliminate; or waited until they were put in a diaper or pull-on for naps or night time before they would have a BM.

Dr. Taubman also found that "interrupting toilet training and having the child return to diapers resulted in the child spontaneously using the toilet for bowel movements within three months in twenty-four of the twenty-seven children."

If your child is simply refusing to use the potty or toilet for BMs, based on this study, going back to diapers may be a choice you would want to consider. In one of his other studies, they concluded that the behavior of hiding while defecating before completion of toilet training is associated with stool toileting refusal, constipation and stool withholding.

In the child readiness section (emotional growth and social awareness) of this book we discuss the fact that some children like to hide when defecating. The median age of children who start hiding to defecate is 22 months. So, if your child likes to hide when defecating, you need to know that your child may be more likely to resist doing BMs in the potty or toilet and you may have to deal with BM withholding. Also, do check your child's BMs to make sure that he is not constipated.

A child may exhibit non retentive encopresis, or BM resistance, for several reasons.

1. The child is simply not ready i.e. the child is not developmentally ready to be potty trained (see the child readiness section).

2. The child may be afraid to use the toilet.

3. The child may have disruptive behavioral problems such as aggression, oppositional behavior non compliance or temper tantrums.

4. The child may have irritable bowl syndrome.

The first step in dealing with non retentive encopresis is to try and determine why the child is withholding. Consult with your doctor and your child's pediatrician to determine the reason.

Dealing With Bowel Movement Resistance Or Non Retentive Encopresis

Once you and your doctor have determined the reason for the BM resistance, you can plan out a course of action.

If your child is simply not ready, waiting a few months may be just what she needs. In the meantime, take the time to prepare yourself and your child and try again in a few months.

If your child has disruptive behavioral issues, then these behaviors are probably not only manifested in potty training, but also in other areas of her life such as bedtime, bath time, dressing etc. These behaviors need to be addressed by a professional, before potty training.

If your child has irritable bowel syndrome, your doctor may refer you to a specialist for treatment options.

Most children who resist going in the potty are simply afraid. Based on my research and understanding of this issue, many of the children seem to develop a fear of using the toilet. Many a time, the parents don't know how or why the child is afraid; they just see the result i.e. the unwillingness of the child to try and go on the potty.

Pediatrician, Dr. Alan Greene refers to this as D3 cycle – Discomfort, Dread and Delay. A child could easily enter this cycle when potty training. The change in a child's routine could cause the child to hold back a BM, which leads to a painful BM, which leads to holding back even more, thus entering the D3 cycle. If as a parent, you are not aware of the issues with bowel movement when potty training, your child could enter this cycle, causing BM training to be more challenging. Avoid the connection in the child's brain that says that diapers/pull-ons are good – potty training underwear is bad.

In order to move forward in bowel movement training, the D3 cycle must first be broken. According to Dr. Taubman's study, the simplest way to break the D3 cycle may be to go back to diapers or to use diapers or pull-ons for bowel movements. The risk remains that you will undo the potty training, especially the urine training. Another risk is that you create a positive association between diapers and BM in your child's mind.

One of the reasons a child has hard BM is because the child is tense due to all of the changes in his routine, and going back to diapers will release the tension, therefore softening up the BM. If the BMs are not softening, then consider using a stool softener. Consult your child's pediatrician for what you should use. Products available over the counter in the laxative section of your local drug store include Milk of Magnesia, Mineral Oil, Metamucil or Citrucel.

Dr. Greene recommends mineral oil; the mineral oil makes the stools slippery enough that the child can no longer hold it and soft enough so that the bowel movement will not be painful. Mineral Oil has no flavor; it is just thick and slippery in texture. The best way to get your child to take mineral oil is to mix it with food. Blend it in a beverage such as a smoothie or a milkshake, but serve it quickly before it separates. Also you can try using it as a substitute for butter or mayo on bread.

Once the 3D cycle is broken, get back to bowel movement training in small steps.

First, encourage your child to poop in the bathroom. If your child wants a diaper to poop in, give her the diaper, but encourage her to go poop in the bathroom, instead of hiding elsewhere. Once you have established a routine with BMs in the bathroom for three or more days, take the next step.

Try having her sit with her diaper or pull-on while she is having the BM. She can sit right on top of the toilet with the lid down or on the floor or wherever she chooses in the bathroom; you just want to get her used to having a BM while sitting. Once she has mastered having BMs while sitting, move her to be sitting on the potty or the toilet.

After she is comfortable with sitting on the potty or toilet, it is time for the next step — removing the diaper. If your child is not comfortable with this, try cutting a hole in the diaper or leaving the diaper open. You basically want to work your child up to the point of using the potty or the toilet, but you need to take small steps and get comfortable with each step.

Remember, that this behavior is based on fear. Think about how you react when you are afraid. You have to enable your child to get over his fear. You know your child best, so adapt this based on your child. Some children will breeze through it, while others will need a lot of time and many baby steps. Be patient and you will both get there.

SECTION VII

Bed Wetting

Bed wetting is a common problem that affects five to six million children. At the age of 5 years, 15-20 percent of children are still wetting at night two to three times per month. At the age of 6, about 15 percent are still wetting, and 10 percent of children over 7 years of age are still wetting. These rates go down only by about 15 percent per year without treatment. At the age of 15, about 1-2 percent of adolescents still wet at night. There are two types of bed wetting or nocturnal enuresis.

1. Primary nocturnal enuresis is the term used when children have never achieved night time control and are wetting more than 2-3 times per month.

2. Secondary nocturnal enuresis is when a child has been dry at night for 6 months and then begins to wet again. Secondary nocturnal enuresis is easier to treat, because in most cases this is a result of a change in the child's life. Identifying the change and addressing it will resolve the issue in most cases. The change may be situational such as a change in eating, drinking or sleeping habits. It could be physical, such as the onset of diabetes or a urinary track infection or it could be psychological such as a divorce, death, move, birth of new sibling etc.

Treating Primary Nocturnal Enuresis

Most children who wet at night have primary nocturnal enuresis and research indicates that this is indeed hereditary. Researchers have identified three genes named ENUR1, ENUR2 and ENUR3 that have all been associated with primary nocturnal enuresis.

If you were a bed wetter, then your child has a 50 percent chance of being a bed wetter, also. If you and your spouse were both bed wetters, then your child has a 75 percent chance of being a bed wetter. If neither one of you was a bed wetter, your child still has a 15 percent chance of being a bed wetter.

This issue is hard on the children as well as the parents. Parents feel that the fault is theirs because they may not be parenting properly. In some cases parents think that the child is too lazy to go to the bathroom at night. Children feel awful when they wet, especially as they get older. Some may feel that this is happening because they are not doing something right.

There are a number of reasons that children have to urinate at night:

1. Their bodies have not transitioned to only needing to urinate during waking hours.
2. The signal from their brain to wake up and to go potty has not fully matured.
3. They sleep too deeply to be awakened by this signal – this is referred to as "arousal dysfunction."
4. There is imbalance in the bladder muscles — i.e. the muscle that contracts to squeeze the urine out is much stronger than the muscle that holds the urine in.
5. The bladder is too small to hold the normal amount of urine.
6. They produce more urine than a normal size bladder can hold.
7. They drink too much liquid before bed.
8. They may be consuming a diuretic substance such as chocolate or colas that increase the urine output.
9. Constipation might be reducing bladder capacity.
10. It could be a medical issue such as diabetes, a urinary track infection (especially in girls), a hormonal imbalance, or Sickle Cell Anemia.
11. Allergy to milk or other food sensitivities.

What to do if your child has not achieved night time control and is still wetting at night past the age of five.

One of the first things I would recommend is discussing this with your child's pediatrician or better yet, a pediatrician that is skilled in treating bed wetting. Based on your child's history, a physical exam and tests, the child's pediatrician should be able to determine the cause and should be able to recommend a treatment option. Call the National Kidney Foundation at 1-800-622-9010 for referral to a pediatrician in your area who has a special interest in treating bed-wetting.

Treatment Options For Bed Wetting

I have researched this topic, and based on my understanding and knowledge; here are some of the treatment options and therapies that your child's pediatrician may recommend. The goal of all the therapies is to teach the child to wake up when the bladder is full and/or to decrease the need for nighttime urination.

Behavioral Therapies

There are a number of different behavioral therapies such as motivation programs with star charts, guided imagery and hypnosis. Behavioral treatment is often more effective and certainly is safer than medical treatment. While behavioral treatment may take somewhat longer to show results, the improvement usually continues indefinitely. There are several methods that may be helpful:

Imipramine (Janimine, Tofra body and mind will get used to

Imipramine comes in tablet f weeks, the child will master night

evening. It is not known exactly d to use an alarm.

affect the muscles of the bladde

more lightly or may work sim **edication**

Imipramine works best f

ful for children who have n y prescribe medication as a last resort.

have frequent day time we tr increase the amount of urine that the

cent of children treated der capacity) or decrease the amount of

bed wetting for a short idneys. They are used to temporarily con-

pramine have long term as a treatment to completely stop the con-

Imipramine has a

overdose can resultions are ideal for situational use and work well

pramine is on the dental wetting for short periods of time, such as

have less severe sire on overnight trips or at camp. In some cases,

tive.   ons are used along with other behavioral and con-

pies to control bed wetting. Medications are not

Desmopre with younger children, especially with children un-

DDAVP of 5 as they may achieve night time control as they

medication is

also know are three types of medicines that are generally used to

functions d wetting. They are:

producti

reduces   Imipramine (Janimine, Tofranil)

night y   Desmopressin (DDAVP, Stimate)

R 3.   Oxybutynin (Ditropan)

is us

tab

Motivation Programs

These are based on the concept that children wake up easier when the day holds promise and excitement — i.e. it is easier to get out of bed on Christmas morning, or on a day of a major event, especially when compared to a "normal" day. So, this anticipation and excitement is created with a Star Chart – where the child receives a star for each dry night. After three, five or seven nights, the child is given a smaller reward and then after three weeks, the child gets the big prize which is something he really wants.

The prize should be something that will keep the child's excitement and anticipation going for three weeks, because it generally takes that long to break an old habit and form a new one.

These star charts can be used alone or in conjunction with a bed wetting alarm. This motivational program is enough for some children to help them and their bodies learn to be responsive to a full bladder. Always consult your child's pediatrician before starting any therapy program. The program should be modified (i.e. add/remove therapies and tools) if no results are seen in two weeks. Visit www.Potty-Training-in-One-Day.com to print out fun and motivation star chart/calendars.

Guided Imagery

This should be done by a trained professional, but parents can also try this with their child. It basically involves creating a detailed image in your child's mind about how urine is made and how it is eliminated. Dr. Alan Greene recommends the following imagery:

SECTION VIII

Potty Training Summary

I recently talked with a mother of five boys. The first four boys were a breeze to potty train, however, her fifth – the baby of the family, was proving to be quite the challenge when it came to potty training. So, remember that each child is unique and some will train easily while others will take some time. I would like to leave you with these two things:

1. Most children want to be potty trained as much as the parent wants them to be potty trained.

2. Your child deeply cares what you think of him or her and will go out of his or her way to please you – the parent.

When your child is struggling with potty training, it is probably because all of the dots have not been connected in your child's head. Children are unable to articulate the problems they have with our parenting techniques. They cannot verbally communicate that they do not understand what is expected, or if they do understand, they cannot yet control their bodies and make them do what they, and you would like their little bodies to do. So, instead what you see are the results, i.e. resistance or accidents. These are your clues and you have to play detective to find out the root cause and fix the problem.

Put yourself in your toddler's shoes. You are asking your child to learn a lot and then consistently follow through each time. Like all the skills you have taught, encouraged and nurtured so far, such as walking, eating, and talking, potty training is also a skill that requires you to teach your toddler to pay attention to his or her physical needs, think ahead, focus and plan the use of the potty or toilet. Figure out which of these steps is not clear to your child and then work on that step. I guarantee that sooner or later, your child will lose the diapers.

What's most important is that in doing so, your child will feel like a competent, good little boy or girl, and will not feel belittled, diminished, or shamed by the process. Those feelings can persist long after the potty wars have become an amusing episode in your family's history. Look at potty training as another big milestone in your child's life and make it an opportunity to create memories that you will treasure for years. You never know what this potty training adventure could lead to. For me, it led to my third career eight years after I potty trained my boys!

About The Author

Narmin Parpia is mother of two boys who were potty trained in one day. While watching the Dr. Phil show on "How to Potty Train your Child in One Day," Narmin was reminded of how well this method works and how challenging it had been to purchase all the tools (especially the doll) necessary to get the job done. Dr. Phil inspired her to develop anatomically correct drink and wet-on-demand™ dolls and a full line of potty training products  *Potty Scotty*™ for boys and  *Potty Patty*™ for girls.

Narmin holds a degree in chemical engineering. She spent the first few years of her career working at a refinery and then moved to her second career in information technology. Now, she is working on her third career of inventor, mompreneur, business woman and author!

Potty Scotty™ and *Potty Patty*® products have been featured on TV, on the radio, in magazines and newspapers including the Today Show and TIME Magazine. For more information, visit www.Potty-Training-in-One-Day.com.